THE SEASONS OF CUMBERLAND ISLAND

THE SEASONS OF
Cumberland Island

FRED WHITEHEAD

WITH AN INTRODUCTION BY

C. RONALD CARROLL AND DAVID DALLMEYER

THE UNIVERSITY OF GEORGIA PRESS   ATHENS AND LONDON

Published by the University of Georgia Press

Athens, Georgia 30602

www.ugapress.org

Set in 11 on 18 Adobe Garamond with Frutiger

Printed and bound by Sung In Printing

The paper in this book meets the guidelines for

permanence and durability of the Committee on

Production Guidelines for Book Longevity of the

Council on Library Resources.

Printed in Korea

12 11 10 09 08 C 6 5 4 3 2

Library of Congress Cataloging-in-Publication Data

Whitehead, Fred, 1943–

The seasons of Cumberland Island / Fred Whitehead

with an introduction by C. Ronald Carroll and David Dallmeyer.

p. cm. — (A Wormsloe Foundation nature book)

Includes index.

ISBN 0-8203-2497-3 (hardcover : alk. paper)

1. Natural history—Georgia—Cumberland Island.

2. Natural history—Georgia—Cumberland Island—Pictorial works.

3. Cumberland Island (Ga.)—Pictorial works.

I. Title. II. Series.

QH105.G4W46 2004

508.758'746'0222—dc22   2003027909

ISBN-13 978-0-8203-2497-5

British Library Cataloging-in-Publication Data available

TO MY DAUGHTER, STELLA

CONTENTS

Photographer's Preface

FRED WHITEHEAD

I have been privileged to serve as a national park ranger and interpretive naturalist on Cumberland Island for more than two decades. Living and working on Cumberland has allowed me to experience this relatively undeveloped barrier island in a unique and rewarding way. Living here has also allowed me to capture the island's natural beauty on film and to study and document the island's various biological processes over a long period of time. I have, therefore, been able to see firsthand how the different natural environments on Cumberland are regulated by seasonal changes and how these changes affect the area's diverse flora and fauna. This book is an intimate look at Cumberland as I know it, a barrier island many consider to be America's most beautiful.

Because so much of Cumberland stays green throughout the year, most people think of it as subtropical. It is, however, located where the subtropical influences of nearby Florida overlap with elements of the southern temperate zone. This position creates a species-rich biological transition area and means that subtle, yet important, seasonal changes regulate the various natural components of the island. I chose to start the book with autumn because ecologically it is an active time of year and artistically it provides a colorful beginning for this seasonal journey through the environments of Cumberland Island.

Over the years I have come to realize just how important barrier islands are to the health of our coastal and marine life. Like most barrier islands, Cumberland has a long history of human use and impact. Unlike most of them, however, it has been allowed to return to a relatively natural condition. Cumberland Island stands as one of the most, if not the most, ecologically intact barrier islands off the eastern shore of North America. As such, it sets a standard for them all. Cumberland is also a very important link in the chain of islands along the East Coast. It is a refuge for migratory animals, especially birds, and as such has ties to the far reaches of the globe. It is also a large but fragile island that can be seriously impacted not only by what humans do on the island but also by human development in the surrounding areas.

I hope that my words will provide others with a better understanding of how natural processes have created the ecological diversity of Cumberland Island, how some of its many plant and animal species interact, and how the local natural systems respond to seasonal changes. I hope that my photographs will convey the rare beauty and power of the island's different habitats and its native fauna and flora. And finally, I hope that both my words and images will inspire all of us to continue to value and protect Cumberland Island as a natural preserve for future generations to experience and enjoy.

THE SEASONS OF CUMBERLAND ISLAND

What Makes Cumberland Island Special?

C. RONALD CARROLL AND DAVID DALLMEYER

Among North America's barrier islands, Cumberland Island has the largest and most ecologically intact ecosystem. From the expansive oceanfront beaches through the dune complex, interior forests, freshwater ponds, tidal creeks, and salt marshes on the sheltered mainland side of the island, Cumberland is a cross section of all the environments found on large barrier islands. Because so many barrier islands have lost their natural ecosystems to overdevelopment, the natural environment of Cumberland Island takes on special value for its rareness.

Found along shallow coastlines throughout the world, barrier islands play an important environmental role by protecting coasts from severe storms and by sheltering salt marshes that are critically important nurseries for fish, shrimp, and crabs. Such islands are also fascinating and dynamic ecosystems in their own right.

Barrier islands form a necklace of long thin islands off Virginia and the Carolinas to the north and Florida to the south. In the middle of the necklace, off the coast of Georgia, the barrier islands are high and wide. Cumberland Island, at 23,268 acres and 17.5 miles long, is the southernmost of Georgia's barrier islands. It

is also the largest above the high-tide line. Along Georgia's coast, Ossabaw, St. Catharine, Sapelo, and Cumberland are the only large barrier islands that have retained substantive pieces of the original barrier-island ecosystem. Of these, Cumberland is by far the most ecologically intact. Since 1972 Cumberland Island has been protected as part of the National Seashore of the National Park System. About 90 percent of the island is protected public land, and the remaining private land has been kept in a relatively natural state.

More than forty thousand people visit Cumberland Island each year despite its limited access by boat. They come to experience the natural beauty of the island and to observe the abundant and diverse plant and animal life. The interior forests include pine, cedar, and hickory trees, but perhaps most impressive are the expansive live oaks, whose twisting branches are draped with Spanish moss. Underneath the trees, saw palmetto and resurrection ferns thrive in the shade. Muscadine vines hang from tree branches, providing fruit for birds and other animals. Deer, turkeys, and rac-

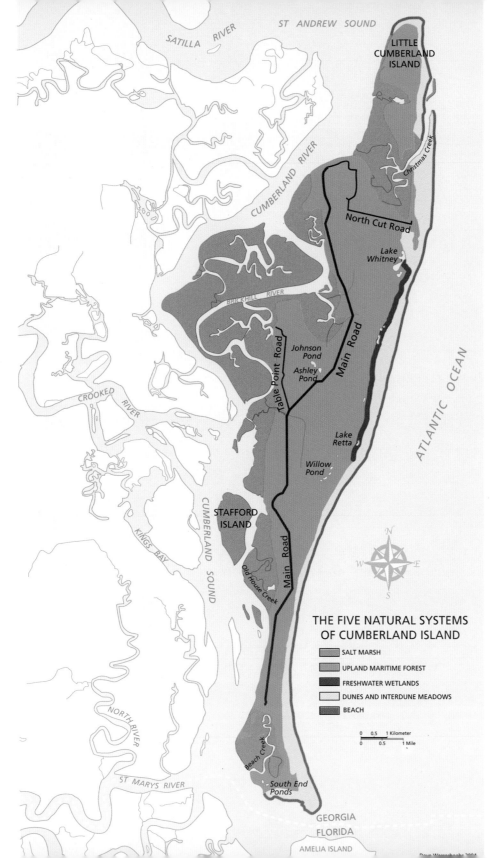

**THE FIVE NATURAL SYSTEMS
OF CUMBERLAND ISLAND**

- SALT MARSH
- UPLAND MARITIME FOREST
- FRESHWATER WETLANDS
- DUNES AND INTERDUNE MEADOWS
- BEACH

coons roam the forest. Great horned owls nest here, and songbirds break the silence of the woods. Among the dunes sea oats and muhly grass with its purple flowers grow. Shorebirds are plentiful, as are horseshoe crabs. And in the expansive salt marsh otters hunt for mullet, while wood storks and egrets search among the mudflats and oyster beds at low tide for fiddler crabs and small fish.

THE FORMATION OF BARRIER ISLANDS

The ocean-facing beach of Cumberland provides clues indicating that the seaward side of this massive island was once a very different environment. Scattered along the dunes are the skeletons of trees, their blanched limbs and trunks testimony to the abrasive effects of windblown sand. These were once live oaks and other components of an inland forest, but now they are isolated shore relics. There are also table-sized patches of dark organic mats concealing tangles of roots. These mats are root masses of Spartina marsh grass, which form part of the salt marsh on the mainland side of the island and along tidal creeks. Spartina does not grow along the exposed beach. Shells that once contained living animals, such as oysters, can be found in the brackish intertidal zone, which is their natural habitat. Taken together, these clues reveal that the oceanfront beach was once interior forest or salt marsh situated between the barrier island and the mainland.

The location of Cumberland Island, like all barrier islands, is slowly changing. Because sea level is rising, Cumberland is gradually rolling toward the coastline. Sediments from the Satilla River maintain a large delta known as Little Cumberland Island. A series of ridges occur on the northern end of Cumberland Island. This expanding part of Cumberland has been built up from sediments washed down by rivers from the Piedmont. Winter is the best season to appreciate these changes, because strong winter waves and the strong southward current at this time expose older formations beneath the beach; it is possible to see where parts of the island shore are eroding while other parts are growing.

What conditions are necessary for barrier islands to form? Along the Atlantic coast such islands, including Cumberland, need a gently sloping beach and subtidal zone, a longshore current to transport sand, a source of new sand, and a rising sea level.

GLACIAL ORIGINS

Cumberland Island really began forming during the height of the most recent global ice age, when the edge of the ocean was forty to fifty miles east of where it is now. About eighteen thousand years ago, the glaciers began to melt and retreat, causing a rapid rise in sea level. Cumberland Island formed and began rolling westward toward the coastline. Although the movement would have seemed imperceptible, the island was turning over too quickly for permanent vegetation cover to become established. As the rate of sea level rise began to slow about five thousand years ago, Cumberland's movement slowed, and the characteristic maritime forest and other island vegetation established itself, creating the environment we see today.

PROTECTIVE SANDBARS

Sandbars associated with Cumberland's coast illustrate the continuously shifting nature of beaches and shallow sediments. With powerful storms and the strong southward current of winter, sand is pulled off the beaches and accumulated in offshore bars. Waves undercut the seaward side of the sandbars and pull them out to sea. During the winter season the bars move farther offshore, where they are defined by a distant line of breaking waves. The sandbars migrate back toward shore during the summer, when gentle waves and weak northward shore currents add to the beachfront.

Sandbars play an important role in protecting barrier islands by absorbing wave energy that would otherwise continuously erode the beachfront. The interplay between sandbar formation in the winter and beach expansion in the summer keeps barrier-island beaches in dynamic equilibrium.

THE ROLE OF DUNES

Dunes also have a critical role in protecting the integrity of barrier islands. Dunes, which require plant cover—especially sea oats—to hold them together, provide protection against strong storm surges that would otherwise overwash barrier islands more frequently than they do and make the islands less stable. Because the dual processes of erosion and sediment addition can easily be disrupted, the stability of dunes is crucial.

Humans can have an impact on dune stability. When people walk across the crest of a dune, they create a V-shaped notch in the top of that dune. Onshore winds funnel through these small notches with increased velocities. As a consequence, dune sand begins to blow away, and the notch becomes deeper and wider. Soon the

lands. Because beach erosion represents a large economic loss for tourism and real-estate values, people have gone to great efforts to prevent beach sands from eroding and to replenish beaches by pumping sands from offshore onto the beach. Beach stabilization structures such as groins and jetties interrupt normal shoreline erosion and interfere with longshore sand transport. In fact, almost every such effort to save beaches simply creates greater loss of sand for beaches down current.

THE PULSING ECOSYSTEM OF THE SALT MARSH

Sheltered between barrier islands and the mainland shore are extensive salt marshes, which are among the most productive ecosystems in the world. Salt marshes form along shallow coastlines where rivers create brackish tides. Along the Georgia coast more than four hundred thousand acres of salt marsh occur between the main shore and the barrier islands, accounting for nearly one-third of all the salt marshes along the Atlantic coast of North America. For Cumberland Island the most extensive salt marsh is between the middle shoreward side of the island and the mainland.

The salt marsh is a harsh and stressful environment. The

sand is swept away faster than the roots of the sea oats can trap the sand. If the process continues, large sections of an oceanfront dune may disappear, and the protection that dunes offer will be substantially reduced.

BEACH EROSION

To many people who are accustomed to seeing erosion of farmlands, riverbanks, and other upland landscapes, erosion has a negative connotation. Not so for barrier-island beaches. Erosion of beaches is part of the dynamic process of adding and subtracting sediment, a natural cycle that maintains the system of barrier is-

muddy bottom is nearly absent of oxygen, summertime surface temperatures are high, and evaporation can produce crystalline layers of salt. Salt-marsh organisms are therefore well adapted to conditions of low oxygen, great diurnal (twenty-four-hour) temperature changes, and high salinity—conditions that would kill and pickle most organisms.

THE LOW MARSH

The salt marsh is a pulsing ecosystem driven by the tidal cycle. Tidal creeks carry the high tide into the marsh and drain the marsh during low tide. The well-known ecologist Eugene Odum likened the tides and tidal creeks to the human circulatory system, with the tides acting as the heart pump and the large and small tidal creeks serving as blood vessels and capillaries. During high tide oxygenated water carrying mineral nutrients is pumped into the marsh; during low tide oxygen-depleted water carrying organic marsh waste is pumped out. Such "waste" contains all the organic matter (detritus) left by dying plants and animals. Some of this organic matter serves as a nutrient base to support bacteria, algae, plankton, and the young stages of various fish and crustaceans in shallow coastal waters. Some organic matter accumulates in the marsh and gradually gives rise to hammock islands. And much of

the organic matter is simply redistributed in the marsh and further broken down by bacteria, diatoms, algae, and many detritus feeders, such as crabs.

The productivity of salt-marsh ecosystems is largely due to one species of spartina grass known as smooth cordgrass. This plant provides food and cover for birds and animals, serves as a protective habitat for certain crustaceans and fish, and filters sediment from saltwater, using nutrients from the sediment. Such species as salt meadow cordgrass and black needle rush are also important contributors to the marsh environment, as are the tiny algae known as diatoms.

The marsh has been described as a great nursery that feeds the young and adults of blue crabs, shrimp, flounder, mullet, oysters, and dozens of other species of ecological if not gastronomic significance. On calm summer nights on an incoming high tide, the marsh is filled with popping sounds. These sounds are the feeding noises made by enormous populations of juvenile shrimp as they graze upon the diatoms and organic detritus.

THE HIGH MARSH

Since the salt marsh is shallow and nearly flat, a small change in elevation translates into striking changes in the marsh ecosystem.

The banks of the tidal creeks that penetrate the marsh are slightly higher than the rest of the low marsh, which is flooded for much of the tidal cycle with a flow of highly oxygenated water. Because the high marsh is exposed for long periods, salt is left on the surface of the soil when the tidal water evaporates. In the high marsh, salt concentrations sometimes exceed even the limits of halophytes (plants that are well adapted to surviving this salty environment), and barren salt pans form.

It would be difficult to exaggerate the importance of Georgia's salt marshes. They remove pollutants that would otherwise enter the coastal food chain, and they support an abundance of economically and ecologically important marine species. Moreover, the great piles of dead marsh plants that wash up on oceanfront beaches during winter storms help to stabilize sand and initiate dune formation.

Cumberland Island and the other barrier islands of Georgia stand sentinel to the state's salt marshes. They protect a natural water-treatment plant that removes pollutants before they enter the coastal ecosystem, an aesthetic waterscape, an economic engine that supports much of our marine fisheries, and an intricate ecological marvel.

THE BIRDS OF CUMBERLAND

Cumberland Island is the year-round home to about 62 bird species. The other 202 species identified on the island are visitors. Arriving during the spring from Mexico, Latin America, and the Caribbean are such songbirds as painted buntings and other migrants from the neotropics. Many of these species will remain to nest and rear young on Cumberland. Other species will stop over on Cumberland to feed on their way to northern or inland breeding areas. Warblers make up more than half of these migrant species. In an amazing feat of endurance, the black-poll warbler, for example, leaves the misty cloud forests of the Andes Mountains in South America and makes a brief spring stopover on Cumberland Island on its way to Arctic breeding grounds, a flight of several thousand miles.

Cumberland is also a wintering area for numerous species of birds. During the spring, the winter residents leave, mostly for more northern or inland regions.

For the birds arriving or departing Cumberland Island, having adequate flight fuel is their most critical need. The tiny ruby-throated hummingbird, for example, flies nonstop across the Gulf

of Mexico, losing about half its weight during the flight. So for many bird species, Cumberland serves as a vital refueling stop on their long migratory journeys of many thousands of miles.

Why leave the tropics at all? Southern temperate-zone forests, including those on Cumberland, have a large flush of insects in the spring that migrants gorge on to replenish nutrients lost during migration and then to rear broods. On the average, temperate-zone breeding birds are able to rear more young than birds that breed in the tropics. The tropical migrants breeding on Cumberland Island gain an advantage in breeding by producing more young.

Surprisingly, the success or failure of migration for many shorebirds is strongly influenced by one species—the ancient horseshoe crab. This species is millions of years old and makes its living by grinding up clams, snails, and worms with burrs at the base of its front legs, which surround its mouth. During early spring the horseshoe crab lays eggs in large numbers above the low-tide line on certain beaches. Shorebirds gorge on the fat-filled crab eggs during their spring migration. Although many shorebirds eat these eggs, at least two—red knots and dunlins—appear to time their migration to the high Arctic to coincide with the egg-laying period of the horseshoe crabs.

Cumberland Island has great ecological significance for many birds, such as the least tern. As its name implies, the nine-inch-long shorebird is the smallest of the fifteen North American terns. A federally protected species, the least tern nests in colonies on shallow wide beaches, just the sort of beach that is in high demand by tourists. Unfortunately, the nesting terns are easily spooked by people or dogs and may abandon their nests. Hogs, raccoons, and opossums also take their toll on least tern eggs and chicks, but disturbances by humans appear to pose the greatest threat.

SEA OATS, BIRD FOOD, AND OAK FORESTS

Plants literally hold Cumberland Island together. Barrier islands are little more than great piles of sand and sediment; they lack a rocky spine to withstand the constant onslaught of tides, waves, and wind. Without the binding effect of plant roots and organic matter, barrier islands would disappear back into the sea. Cumberland's plant communities change along horizontal lines—from oceanfront dune vegetation through interior oak forests in the uplands and sloughs in low-lying areas, to salt-marsh meadows on the mainland side of the island.

For its fundamental contribution to the stability of the island, no plant is more important than the sea oat. This tall grass grows along the oceanfront and on the crest of dunes. The extensive root system of sea oats holds loose sand together, thereby creating dunes and stabilizing them. More complex plant communities establish themselves behind the dunes, which act as a buffer against the ocean.

Wax myrtle forms shrubby thickets throughout the island and enriches the soil for other plants. Barrier-island soils are sandy and deficient in nitrogen; the roots of the wax myrtle support bacteria that convert atmospheric nitrogen into forms that plants can use. Interspersed with wax myrtle are small red bay trees, whose fruits are reminiscent of miniature avocados. The red bay fruit is a high-quality, oil-rich food source for birds, but the fruit season is short. In contrast, the fruit of the wax myrtle is available for a longer period, although the fruit is of a lower quality than that of the red bay.

Oaks, red-fruited hollies, and magnolias are common island trees that also provide food for island wildlife. The large acorns of oak trees are significant food sources for native turkeys and deer. When acorns are scarce, most get eaten. But when acorns are abundant, squirrels hide them here and there, a behavior known as "scatter hoarding," or in common parlance, "squirreling away." When the squirrels do not return for the hidden acorns, they may germinate and grow into the next generation of oak trees.

MARINE LIFE

The waters around Cumberland Island are teeming with marine life. Among the larger marine traffic in the ocean and tidal creeks around the island are the bottle-nosed dolphin, manatee, and loggerhead turtle, which is the only species of sea turtle to nest regularly on Cumberland.

In the wide intertidal zone on Cumberland's ocean side, parchment tube crabs, coquina clams, and olive snails can be seen during low tide on the exposed sand and mud flats. At night the beach is alive with ghost crabs, which scurry along the shoreline as they feed on organic matter during the warmer months.

On the salt-marsh side of the island, scavenging mud snails, periwinkle snails, and oysters abound. The periwinkles are most conspicuous during high tide; they climb up the stems of marsh grass to escape the blue crabs that come into the marsh at high tide to feed. Thousands of tiny fiddler crabs scurry about for food, as well, at low tide. These crabs play an important role by processing coarse organic matter into fine material that becomes food for plankton and contributes to the food web of coastal fisheries.

Many species of oaks grow throughout the island's various ecosystems. Cumberland's signature trees are massive live oaks that fill the canopy over most of the island, but even these large species become small and shrubby when exposed to the harsher environment of the ocean side of the island. Other oak species of the maritime forest—the bluejack, turkey, and myrtle oaks—have adapted to poorer soils and tougher climatic conditions by growing smaller and forming thickets. These plants are part of a scrub habitat on the north end of Cumberland that burns more frequently from lightning-caused fires.

THE TROUBLE WITH HOGS AND HORSES

Some nonnative species to Cumberland, particularly hogs and horses, are destructive forces. A large population of feral hogs eats most of the fall acorn crop. Of the few acorns that survive to germinate, rooting hogs (and some browsing deer) kill most of the young seedlings and saplings. Hogs are particularly efficient foragers because their acute sense of smell helps them locate acorns, even ones that are buried.

Hogs are noted for their long-term memory of the location of particularly desirable foods, and they will return to an area repeatedly until the food is exhausted. Not only caches of acorns but also many understory plants (which grow beneath the shade of trees), snakes, and sea turtles are vulnerable to a hog's prodigious memory. Once a hog develops a taste for turtle eggs, it quickly learns the odor of turtle nests and will return to the nesting beach frequently until no more nests are found. A single hog can easily destroy dozens of nests, causing the deaths of hundreds of developing baby sea turtles.

The wild hogs that cause so much damage to Cumberland's native plants and animals are the descendents of hogs brought by Spanish settlers in the 1600s and domestic swine introduced to the island since colonial times. It was common practice in Europe to let hogs forage freely in forests to fatten on acorns, beechnuts, and other edible plants. The European settlers of early America continued this practice. Today, with the exception of an occasionally lucky alligator and human hunters, hogs face no predators or serious diseases that might control their numbers.

National Park biologists on Cumberland Island would like to eradicate the hogs, but it will be a difficult challenge for such an adaptable, fecund, and smart animal. When hogs are hunted, the

survivors shift their behavior to become more nocturnal and they learn to avoid traps. The control efforts must be relentless, because even a small residual hog population can quickly rebound if eradication efforts are relaxed.

The famous wild horses of Cumberland Island originated from domestic stock released in the early 1900s. These animals feed heavily on sea oats and other dune vegetation. Sea oats and dunes are seriously damaged by the continuous grazing and trampling of the horses.

PRESERVING CUMBERLAND ISLAND

Unlike most of the public beaches along the Atlantic coast that are heavily used by tourists, the protected beaches of Cumberland serve as a major refuge for birds and other threatened coastal species. Much of the coast of Georgia and many of its barrier islands have been heavily developed. Habitat loss, landscape fragmentation and degradation, the proliferation of cell-phone towers (which are hazardous to migratory birds), and global warming are the results of human activities that are endangering the ability of our coastal environments to sustain healthy life support systems. In satellite images Cumberland Island stands out as a green oasis in contrast to the hard edges of development on the nearby coast.

Several government programs have been created to help conserve the last remaining open spaces on these islands. Georgia's Coastal Marshlands Protection Act (1970) and the Shore Protection Act (1992) provide protection for Georgia's coastal natural resources, especially for dunes and beaches. The federal Coastal Zone Management Act (CZMA; 1972) provides federal grants to coastal states if those states invest similar funds in the management and protection of coastal resources. The 1990 amendment to the CZMA requires participating states to develop plans for controlling non-point-source pollution (mostly agricultural and urban runoff) that causes stress on the coastal ecosystem. This is an important recognition that the protection of the coastal ecosystem is dependent on good stewardship of ecosystems upriver.

It is important to remember, however, that legislation cannot provide complete protection of critical resources and therefore cannot replace the role of a vigilant citizenry. Although many measures are already in place to protect Cumberland Island, it is also important for individuals to be good stewards of nature. In order to continue enjoying Cumberland, visitors are urged to support legislative and other efforts to preserve the rare natural environment of Cumberland. By doing so, we can save this national treasure for future generations.

Autumn

Bordering Cumberland Island on its west side are nearly eight thousand acres of salt marsh covered with Spartina grass. Biologically, this marsh is among the richest natural areas on earth.

OVERLEAF
Autumn in the salt marsh becomes apparent when Spartina foliage matures and turns from green to gold. The high nutritional value of this plant is realized when the leaves and stalks die and decompose, eventually becoming a nutrient-rich soup of detritus. Detritus and the microorganisms it supports in turn feed shellfish, crustaceans, and small fish. As the waters begin to cool down, the decomposition of Spartina slows while food production in the marsh decreases.

Oysters feed by filtering nutrients like detritus and planktonic algae from the water that covers them at high tide. These shellfish, which form large beds in salt-marsh creeks, can remain alive out of the water during periods of low tide and provide feeding areas for other animals.

A river otter makes use of an exposed oyster bed as it comes ashore to eat a fish. By late autumn, as the water cools down, vast numbers of schooling fish move out of the marshes into deeper water or migrate to warmer areas farther south. In turn, otters, which feed mainly on fish, become more active in their search for food.

The highly adaptive raccoon hunts the marsh at low tide for whatever it can find to make a meal. The omnivorous raccoon eats a wide variety of plant and animal life throughout the island. The shoreline where the salt marsh meets the higher forested land, however, shows the heaviest concentration of raccoon activity.

OPPOSITE

Oyster beds and salt-marsh creeks are favored feeding areas for wading birds. Among them are the wood storks, North America's only native stork. In recent years the number of wood storks has drastically declined due to the destruction of habitat in other parts of its range. On Cumberland, wood storks, along with ibis, egrets, and herons, find secure habitat and an abundance of small fish and crustaceans to feed on, even as the waters turn cooler.

Grasses, shrubs, and trees that have some degree of salt tolerance grow in thick abundance at the point where the salt marsh joins the island. These transition zones are typically areas that support a rich diversity of life forms.

Cumberland has more than fifteen thousand acres of high ground, mostly covered by maritime forest. At least fifty species of native trees grow here, but the live oaks dominate the forest. They not only thrive in this climate zone but also can withstand the wind and salt spray better than competing species.

The tops of these trees are sheared and pruned by the forces of wind and salt spray.

OPPOSITE
Oaks close to the beach show the effects of prevailing easterly winds in their stunted, twisted trunks leaning to the west.

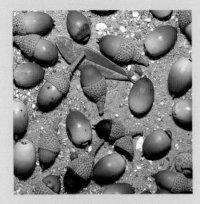

A thick forest canopy covers most of Cumberland throughout all seasons of the year. Live oaks, the predominant canopy cover, do not drop their leaves in autumn but hold the characteristic evergreen foliage typical of subtropical plants. They do, however, produce a fall crop of acorns, an important food source for island wildlife.

White-tailed deer depend on the nutrient-rich acorn crop for reproductive success. Antlered bucks search for receptive does during the "fall rut." They are the largest of as many as twenty species of native land mammals that inhabit Cumberland.

Hogs feed heavily on the fall acorn crop, competing with indigenous wildlife for this vital food source. They also destroy many plant species as they root for food, interrupting the plant successions of the island's habitats. Ground-dwelling populations of fauna, like beneficial snakes, are also placed at risk by the aggressive hogs.

Island hogs breed throughout the year, producing large litters of young. Frequent hunting of this invasive animal is necessary to maintain the biodiversity and stability of island ecosystems.

Feral hogs were first introduced to North America in the 1500s as a dependable and mobile food source for European explorers. The Cumberland Island hogs are the legacy of these hogs and free-range domestic stock.

The eastern diamondback rattlesnake is one of three venomous species found on Cumberland Island, along with the canebrake rattlesnake and the cottonmouth. Rattlesnakes can be found anywhere on the island, but they prefer areas of thick vegetation. They are beneficial controls on rodent populations, which can transmit diseases to other animals, including humans.

OPPOSITE
Cumberland is home to fifteen other species of snakes. The tree-climbing red rat snake is one of the many nonvenomous species found on the island. Snakes and other reptiles become less active as autumn temperatures begin to drop.

The shorter, cooler days bring color to plants of temperate origins, creating a bright counterpoint to the evergreen background of subtropical species. A sabal palm supports the vines of muscadine grape and Virginia creeper, among the first plants to change color in the autumn.

OPPOSITE
By late autumn pignut hickory trees stand out brightly against a mostly green upland subtropical forest. The tree is known as "pignut" because free-ranging hogs consume large quantities of the nuts produced by these hickories this time of year. Hickory trees are sensitive to salt spray, so they grow only on the more protected western side of the island.

Spanish moss keeps its gray foliage throughout the year but becomes colorful and illuminates the forest when backlit by an autumn sunset. This distinctive hanging plant is not a moss or a parasite but a subtropical epiphyte that uses trees for support. It can absorb much more than its own weight in rainwater, releasing it slowly into the forest through evaporation, providing other plants with much-needed moisture during dryer periods.

OPPOSITE
A series of natural depressions located between the grown-over remnants of ancient dunes creates a system of interior ponds, marshes, and wooded swamps. Fed by rain, this freshwater resource provides important wetland habitat for a large number of species, including the water-tolerant red maple. Tannic acid from fallen plant material darkens the water, making it highly reflective. Cumberland has nearly seven hundred acres of freshwater wetlands.

Sand, wind, and plants interact to create the elaborate dune systems along the ocean side of Cumberland. The beauty of sea oats in autumn light belies the key functional role this species plays in dune stabilization. Long networks of roots anchor sand in place, while vertical stalks and leaves slow the migration of sand from the surface of the dunes in the struggle against erosion.

Over time, interdune meadows developed between the older dunes and the line of foredunes that border the beach. This habitat of mainly grasses provides an important feeding area for island wildlife. During the autumn, muhly grass with its purple blooms adds color to the interdune meadows, especially on the northern end of the island. In the course of natural succession, these areas will be taken over by woody shrubs and trees.

Foredunes are the most recently established dunes and work with the adjoining beach as a flexible barrier against the sea. This area supports only a few plant species that can live in near-desertlike conditions, among them the Spanish bayonet. The foredunes also provide habitat for both resident and migratory animals.

The undisturbed shoreline of Cumberland provides an important feeding and resting area for migratory birds. Enormous flocks of tree swallows make rest stops here during their fall migration. At least 323 species of birds have been identified on Cumberland; 264 species are either regular visitors or full-time residents.

Cumberland's wide, gradually sloping beach absorbs wave energy and protects the island from the forces of the sea. This is especially important during the late fall and winter storm season.

Winter

OVERLEAF
Winter storms are part of the dynamics that
shape the island. Higher than normal tides,
driven by northeast storms, cut into the
foredunes and pull sand from the beach.
Wind and wave action churn tannic acid and
organic material from nearby salt marshes
and coastal rivers into thick sea foam.

Calm before the storm—advancing weather fronts are a common sight from Cumberland's beach in the winter. The direction and velocity of the wind have dramatic effects on the island's shoreline during this season.

Rough seas dislodge many varieties of seashells and other forms of marine life from the shallow offshore bottom. Because of the island's location, both tropical and temperate species are found washed up on Cumberland's beaches. During the calmer summer months, sand lost during winter storms will be gradually redeposited on the beach.

Dead stalks of Spartina grass from the salt marsh behind the island are carried by the tides into the ocean and deposited on the beach.

This mat of vegetation known as "marshwrack" traps windblown sand and helps repair existing dune lines.

Marshwrack provides sea oats and other pioneer plants a place to anchor, enabling new dune systems and the adjoining beach to gain ground against the sea.

OPPOSITE
Dunes are the island's most prominent geological feature. They reach elevations of more than fifty feet in some areas.

During strong northerly storms the importance of vegetation becomes obvious, as loose surface sand not covered with vegetation moves or "migrates" rapidly with the wind.

OPPOSITE
Dune migration caused by strong winds will often push destabilized dunes into the forest, smothering trees to death by cutting off the supply of oxygen to the root systems.

Winter is mostly a dry season; however, wet-weather fronts can bring enough rain to fill natural depressions behind the dunes and in the interdune meadows. Excessive rainwater will breach the dunes and flow onto the beach.

OPPOSITE
By spring, standing freshwater becomes a breeding area for insects and other small aquatic animals, thereby creating a food chain that leads to larger animals.

Located on the Atlantic flyway, Cumberland serves as an important wintering area for waterfowl. Migratory hooded mergansers spend most of the winter season in the salt marshes, where they feed mainly on small fish. During cold, windy weather these ducks will cautiously enter the island's interior tidal creeks to seek shelter.

The intertidal creeks and salt marshes host an abundance of animals. Seldom seen are mink. These animals are nocturnal most of the year, but in winter they become active during daylight hours as well. Mink prey heavily on small fish and have adapted well to the salt-marsh environment. Winter is the breeding season for these tireless members of the weasel family, and they will cover large areas in search of mates. Mink can move about more freely during the winter, when their main predator, the alligator, is inactive.

Coastal fog is another weather condition that becomes part of Cumberland's winter character. Deer move cautiously in the poor visibility of a thick morning fog, constantly on the lookout for their main island predator, the bobcat.

Well-camouflaged with a winter coat, a bobcat surveys its island domain. Bobcats are native to the region but were probably extirpated from Cumberland in the early 1900s. Since their reintroduction to the island in 1988, these effective predators have benefited the deer herd by helping to keep them from overpopulating and overfeeding their range. Bobcats also prey on a host of other mammals, including marsh rabbits, raccoons, pigs, and small rodents.

Spring

The lives of animals that inhabit the beach area are influenced mainly by the tides. American oystercatchers probe the exposed beach for mollusks on a falling tide. In the late spring they nest on the beach above the high-tide line.

OPPOSITE
As the shallow waters along the beach warm up during the spring, marine animals move in close to find food and to breed. Horseshoe crabs feeding on bottom-dwelling invertebrates often get stranded on the beach at low tide. Some of these slow-moving animals become beached as a result of northeast storms that occur into the early spring.

OVERLEAF
Migratory shorebirds, such as red knots, depend on Cumberland's long, undisturbed beach for feeding and resting areas during their spring migration.

Spring begins during the windy month of March, but by April a calmness settles in as the island starts to "green up."

Many neotropical birds migrate north to Cumberland in the spring, and the male painted bunting is the most colorful bird to visit the island. Cumberland provides suitable nesting grounds for buntings, along with nearly one hundred other species. Buntings begin nesting in the forest during springtime and feed mainly on grass seeds and insects along the edges of wooded areas. Unfortunately, bunting populations are declining rapidly due to the destruction of their habitats in Florida.

The live oaks, which kept their leaves through the winter, show signs of new life. As the old leaves drop, new light-green leaves and pollen heads immediately take their place, hence the name "live oak."

Pileated woodpeckers, the largest of seven species of woodpecker found on the island, are provided an excellent nesting site by a decaying tree. Wood-boring insects that become active on trees in the spring are their main food source.

Unlike most of Cumberland's bird life, wild turkeys do not migrate with the seasons. They do, however, feed regularly at the edge of the forest this time of year on new plant growth and a variety of insects. Turkeys also use the open areas for courtship displays.

OPPOSITE
Spring is the breeding season for wild turkeys. Males put on showy courtship displays in the early morning light to attract females for mating.

OPPOSITE
Deer feed mostly at the edge of the forest, where sunlight can produce new plant growth within reach. Fawns are born in the spring, when food is plentiful.

The most noticeable animals on the island are the free-ranging feral horses, which prefer the open grassy areas to feed on. Today's island horses originated from domestic stock released in the early 1900s. Attracted by new spring growth, horses graze and trample the salt marsh, seriously impacting this vital marine nursery area.

OPPOSITE
In the late spring, horses visit the beach to seek relief from biting insects.

During this time of year the horses feed heavily on sea oats and other dune vegetation. Sea oats become seriously damaged by the continuous grazing and trampling of the horses. With less plant cover, dunes erode and migrate, thereby threatening the stability of the shoreline and other island ecosystems.

OPPOSITE
In the wild, horses form family groups led by a dominant stallion that rigorously defends his herd of mares and the territory they occupy.

The freshwater wetlands show a great diversity of new plant growth in the spring, as this system is dramatically undergoing the various stages of plant succession. Open ponds naturally fill in with emergent aquatic plants and eventually become swamps and lowland forest. Rapid dune migration exacerbated by the grazing of introduced species is altering the natural succession of plants and animals in some of these wetland areas.

As the spring sunshine warms the island waters, fish return to shallow areas to feed. This is when fish-eating birds can capture enough food to rear their young. Great egrets and other wading birds nest in rookeries among the freshwater wetlands. To provide security from nest-raiding raccoons, they prefer building their nests in trees surrounded by water that is habitat for alligators.

As air and water temperatures rise, cold-blooded animals become active, including alligators, the island's largest predators. These opportunistic feeders eat all forms of animal life. As spring progresses, water levels usually recede, causing animals to concentrate in and around water holes, where they are easy prey for alligators. Alligators will also enter tidal creeks and salt marshes to search for food but will eventually return to freshwater. Spring is also the time of year when wetland sounds include the bellowing of alligators—a prelude to mating.

Summer

Summer brings major weather and biological changes to Cumberland. Spectacular thunderstorms build up and drench the island with sudden downpours.

OVERLEAF
Cumberland's live oaks are home to a host of other species, from ferns and tree frogs to cicadas. The epiphytic resurrection fern curls and shrinks to conserve moisture during dry periods, but within a day after heavy rains it opens up—lush, green, and vibrant—living up to its name.

Over the course of a summer, hundreds of lightning strikes may hit the island. Pine trees are frequently targeted. Fires caused by lightning are necessary to sustain fire-tolerant and fire-dependant plant communities. Periodic fires prevent young competing hardwoods from eventually shading out the more fire-resistant pines. They also facilitate nutrient recycling, kill harmful parasites, and open the forest so that sunlight can reach new growth.

OPPOSITE
The highly adaptable saw palmetto will burn completely to the ground in a forest fire then sprout new growth within a few days. These shade-tolerant palms, which also grow in full sunlight, are the island's most prominent undergrowth species, providing a dense protective cover for many forms of animal life.

Palmettos flower during the summer and produce nutrient-rich berries, a food source for raccoon, deer, and turkey.

The green tree frog is one of at least seventeen species of amphibians found on Cumberland. These moisture-loving animals thrive on the island's humid climate, congregating in large numbers during the summer breeding season. Dependent on moisture for reproduction, male frogs call females while perched on plants near water or break readily into a loud chorus just before a rain shower.

By late summer the annual cicadas produce a deafening mating call of up to one hundred decibels. Females deposit their eggs on tree branches. Upon hatching, the young burrow underground, where they live as nymphs, drawing nourishment from the roots of trees. Within three years they emerge from the ground and transform into another generation of raucous, flying insects.

In the 1920s the nine-banded armadillo was introduced into Florida from Central America. These buoyant swimmers may have been caught by the tides and carried to the island. Armadillos were first recorded on Cumberland in 1974. Members of the anteater family, they root the ground for insects and small reptiles, including snakes. By summer the young, which are always quadruplets of the same sex, emerge from their sandy burrows and forage on their own.

OPPOSITE
The beach side of the foredunes is the outer limit for terrestrial vegetation on the island. This active area, often eroded by winter storms, becomes more stable during the summer as plants grow and spread across the dunes. Railroad vines catch and hold windblown sand, contributing to a stable foredune system that is critical for nesting sea turtles and shorebirds.

Of the five species of sea turtles recorded in the area, almost all of those nesting on Cumberland are loggerheads. Adult female loggerhead turtles, averaging between two and three hundred pounds, leave the water in early summer to nest on Cumberland's rare undisturbed beaches. Preferring moonlit nights, when they can see the silhouette of the shoreline, the females search for a high place to nest in the foredune area. After depositing between 100 and 150 eggs in a nest chamber and carefully covering the nest with packed sand, the mother turtle returns to the sea.

After about sixty days, hatchling sea turtles dig themselves out of the nest and head for the sea. At this time they are able to imprint on their memory the section of beach where they were hatched—they will return to the same area to nest as adults. Cumberland provides key nesting habitat for global species that are losing ground every year on the southeast coast.

By summer the salt marsh is green and full of life. While the salt marsh generates a new crop of Spartina grass, the dead and downed stalks from the previous winter will decompose rapidly in the summer heat, producing a nutrient-rich detritus, the fuel that runs the biological engine in these coastal waters.

One acre of salt marsh can support nearly one million fiddler crabs, one of many species that feed on decomposed organic material. Fiddlers get their name from the large claw of the male crabs. The males use their large claws for courtship displays. These small crabs are an important link in the food chain between detritus and larger animals.

The secretive clapper rail or "marsh hen" is strictly a salt-marsh bird that feeds heavily on fiddlers at low tide. During high tides, rails may seek out floating piles of dead Spartina along the edge of the creeks to keep themselves out of the water.

OPPOSITE
During summertime osprey easily capture striped mullet when they school near the surface of the water in tidal creeks. The large birds take their catch to a nearby island tree to be eaten. Mullet are the marsh's largest detritus-eating animals, and they are an important food source for numerous predators.

Bottle-nosed dolphins represent large animals at the top of the food chain in these coastal waters. They are the most commonly seen sea mammals around Cumberland, as they hunt the maze of salt-marsh creeks and open waters off the beaches.

The subtle seasonal changes on Cumberland are part of an intricate process that influences all of the island's ecosystems. Cumberland Island is an important stronghold for biodiversity and natural beauty in this coastal region. Most of the island belongs to the American people and has been entrusted to the National Park Service. It is a place where both the scientific and aesthetic aspects of nature can be explored and enjoyed away from the heavy human development that is rapidly changing the coastal systems of the Southeast.

INDEX